Exactly My Own Length

OLIVIA McCANNON was born on Mer... Harlesden, London and Belleville, Par... her poems have appeared in intern... ...ns including *Modern Poetry in Translat...* ...*or Life*, *Poems for Love* and the Carcanet Oxfo... ...gy 2007. She has written lyrics and librettos for comp... ...a singers, and her short fiction has been broadcast on Radio 4. ...er translations include Balzac's *Old Man Goriot* (Penguin Classics, 2011), modern French poetry in *Poetry of Place: Paris* (Eland, 2012) and contemporary Francophone plays for the Royal Court theatre in London.

OLIVIA McCANNON

Exactly My Own Length

Oxford*Poets*

CARCANET

First published in Great Britain in 2011 by

Carcanet Press Limited
Alliance House
Cross Street
Manchester M2 7AQ

www.carcanet.co.uk

A CIP catalogue record for this book is available from the British Library

ISBN 978 1 90618 804 7

The publisher acknowledges financial assistance from Arts Council England

Typeset by XL Publishing Services, Tiverton
Printed and bound in England by SRP Ltd, Exeter

For Judith McCannon (1947–2008)

Acknowledgements

Acknowledgements are due to the editors of *Modern Poetry in Translation*, the *Oxford Magazine*, Penguin's *Poems for Life* and Penguin's *Poems for Love*, the OxfordPoets anthology 2007, the *Keats-Shelley Review*, the *Wolf* and *Saw*, in which the following poems first appeared: 'Liverpool Echo', 'City of the Dead', 'Mirror', 'Dust', 'Map', 'Cohabitation', 'Paper Tiger', 'Probability', 'Light-Stone', 'Barometer', 'Unborn', 'Ironing', 'Number 3', 'Exactly My Own Length', 'Book of Hours', 'Laughter', 'Sick World', 'At the Door', 'Honouring the Dead', 'Landing Light', 'Vigil', 'What To Do With a Baby' and 'Fragile Domain'.

Contents

He's not there any more, the man outside Marks and Sparks,
Twice a minute every day for years, he shouted – *'C'o!*

It was always winter and always dark,
His – *'C'o!* was church-loud, hollow and cold.

A blast of mist, shaped by his mouth's warm hole
Into an O as irrevocable as crematorium smoke.

Wiping out the *Socks and Lighters three for a pound Ladies*
As it hacked across the drawn strings of his throat.

A relentless prophet in a worn-thin donkey jacket,
His cover was the smudgy newspaper he sold

Let someone draw his outline on the brick in chalk,
His silence, like his noise was, is that hole

When twilight traced around the skyline
When the lit-up tower restaurant was a place you'd never go

While on the Mersey, ships arrived and left as shadows
And foghorns joined their gloom to his – *'C'o!*

While flurries of starlings kept breaking up the dark –
Singing particle swarms, black hearts numb with cold –

He was always there, the man outside Marks and Sparks,
Twice a minute every day for years, he shouted – *'C'o!*

City of the Dead
Cairo

I live in the shadow of the Sultan's tomb,
He lies in my light. I listen, at dawn
For the voices of his retinue, but
Mum says they spoke louder with their eyes.

No matter: the sitcoms start at nine.
We've got a dish up by the dome
To fish out voices from the ether,
Faces from other worlds and eras.

Dad says we wear the masks of the Dead,
Their blood runs through our veins
Their thoughts run through our heads.
We are invisible, like them.

Tourists don't find us picturesque
Postmen can't find the numberless,
Addresses here are arabesques
And so we live between the lines

Of tombs and sleep on stone and bones
With wives and slaves and dancers.
No big deal. Sultan's pleasure.
We breathe the air that they do not:

Desert air. Infused with drying dust.
It would be clean as death itself
Without us Living with our flesh
Our fumes, our faeces, and our food.

Dust

Most of my life is buried in that room.
I look in through the shattered glass

And see a conversation strobed
Out by the blast. I ran across

This continent so that the dust,
Which fell for years, could not bury the rest.

Mirror

I've got a mirror hanging from my pack
It stares up at the sky. The sky stares back.

The pretty half of my mum's powder compact
We left the rest in a heap, ten miles back.

All gone, the powder that kept her young
Daily facemasks of dust have made us old.

The only thing still pink is my dry tongue
Poking the cavities filled with our last gold.

I can never see more than a piece of my face
Never more than an eye and half a nose.

We've been walking through this waste for days
Wearing the same black as our shadows.

Dad says it must be 40 in the shade.
And no shade anywhere. Walking for days

For days and our bones are dryer than ever,
We skitter like dead leaves across the map.

With all this light we're lighter now than ever
Our packs emptier but heavier now than ever

Every day it is even harder than ever
To open our eyes and let the sand pour in.

Today I stared so hard at the sky it cracked.

Map

On the day they find me,
They'll slit me along my seams
And peel me out of my skin.

They'll dig out a pit for the rest:
White tendons and hashed flesh
Flopped innards full of stink.

What they want is my hide,
They want it beaten flat
The eyes punched in like glass.

Thrashed and stretched and tanned
Until pores show through the sand
And there's five peninsulas to a hand.

Until nipples spread to ridges
And silver-pink scars are rivers
Stitched across with bridges.

When it's taut and dry,
They'll back it onto a grid
Trace on dotted lines

Circle round the ridges
Add crosses for the mines
Rename all the bridges.

Cohabitation

Sometimes it was a bombed-out house
Carpeted with the shards of a meagre life
That the family would walk over with bare feet
Pretending, for the child, to find something to eat

Or an exterminating wind or wall of water
Crushing bodies into its bricks and mortar
Or an eye lined with sticky black flies
And a hand too limp to flick them away

Or the hardened voice, the scarred face
Of a dazed child trailing a sad stump
Which drove them to the plot of wasteland
That used to be our rubbish dump.

We stare at them through bullet-proof glass.
Often they just blur into the background
Until a pillar of smoke, a blast of firecrackers
Remind us we live next to the favela.

Paper Tiger

I queued for three years in the rain outside your door
Shuffling in slippers between barriers, head bowed

To deflect the glare of your guns and windows
Carefully holding the pink and green slips of paper,

The specially sized photos that were asked for
With a centimetre's length between nose and chin.

My face had washed away, my name dissolved
By the time my number showed and you let me in.

Jubilee Portraits

I

Taken fifty years ago in black and white,
Developed with the enlarger he made from a gunsight
On a ship in Kiel, waiting to be demobbed.

Sun shots on the beach at Weston-Super-Mare,
Caravans, ice-cream, donkeys – it's all there:
The proof that their fun is as good as anyone's.

The top one shows she never swims, just paddles.
She will always hold that small hand tight
She will always worry that the tide is going out.

Her job is to show it's best in the shallows.
His is to watch, record, agree
His lips do move, but inaudibly.

The man who repaired the guns but didn't fire them
The man who took the photos but wasn't in them.

II

Their wedding. Him in uniform, just on leave
Her in a coupon dress clutching a bunch of sweet peas
One day in lieu then years spent waiting for peace.

They sent him to Iceland. He was nineteen
He landed in Normandy, crossed Europe to Kiel
Got the odd medal. He was good behind the scenes.

He came home to work at Fry's Chocolate Factory
She gave back her job, stopped playing hockey.

He spent his weekends repairing things –
Radios, dolls – glueing, welding, soldering.

In the shed I found one of him in waders
Fiddling with a warship that he'd made
Taken by the friend he'd asked to hold his Leica
Everything around him shrunk to miniature.

No. 3

Into Number Three they poured
The past, the present and the future
Held in the space between four walls.

The past tied up in the deposit
The present in the sum paid out each week
The future in someone else's pocket.

They owned the same rooms as next door
Walls that stayed lean even in fatter times
Windows too stiff to open for new air.

Hope went into flowers that outgrew borders
Ambition into the hammering in the shed
Happiness into gaps so small it had to bow its head.

Probability

He always tried to make it better
Put it right
To stop it happening at all was best.

Crossing the road he held her small hand
So tightly
Her knuckles turned white with his stress.

On cliff walks he kept her pressed right in
On the inside
Once she walked through a wasps' nest.

Once she jumped out of an upstairs window
She was fine
She wanted to see what can happen.

Argyle Street, 1983

The stone setts ripped from Argyle Street
Were dumped by the council for free
As a heap of odd angles in our drive
On a day when heat stared you in the face.

Clumps of tar – hard as the carapaces
Of cockroaches – sweated and oozed at the edges
Their soft beneaths asking to be scraped off
With a finger and lodge for ever under a nail.

I climbed up on corners, stiff sandals sticking
Air shimmered, a breeze flounced my dress
Clearing the last fadings of smells
Packed down between cracks by wheels and feet

And now dislodged: lathered bits and leather
Salt, cattle, whisky, roker, sole, strong
Soap, coal-dust, slops, stale beer – spit
The passed-beneath-the-tarmac, fixed in black

But with its surface rippling white, like the river.

Barometer

Black seaweed, a straggle, hung on a rusty
Hook fixed in the stone wall of the cottage.
Sand still sticks to it – its highlights glitter
Two girls picked it off the shingle beach –
It has dried out, is dead and brittle.

One girl uses it to tell the weather –
She notes that it makes humidity visible
When it glistens – that rain plumps its skin.
It responds because of physics, not volition –
She finds that interesting.

The other senses how it thirsts for salt
Relives the way the currents sucked it back
How fish gills brushed against it for a thrill
Smells it springing in the cracks of rocks –
She keeps it alive remembering.

The first girl knows that next summer
When she goes back to the shingle beach
When weak rain has dissolved this piece
There'll be a slick of it to pop and slip on
To sniff at and tug free.

The other is sure she won't go back.

Unborn

Once you were a frozen dead girl
I rescued from a lake too late.
I zipped you into my jacket and held you
Against me for hours until I felt
Your warm breath moisten the air again.
We walked into the city –
So many people. But couldn't
Find your parents anywhere.

Another time I had you on a cushion
Under a shawl in a shopping basket,
Birth presents tucked around you.
We were both younger then. I raised
The blanket to watch you as you slept –
Underneath were hard-limbed plastic dolls
With glossy eye-whites and shellac lashes
Staring at the sky behind my back.

Light-Stone

Yesterday, soul,
You went to the sea without me
He saw you in the stone

He saw you in the stone
As my body lay here empty
In the blank space of winter

In the blank space of winter
I lay and held the stone
And he saw you in the sea

He saw you in the sea
The stone sank into me
And I saw the sinking sun

I saw the sinking sun
Reflected on my face
As I lay here in blank space

As I lay here in blank space
With nothing to hold onto but
This stone showing light

This stone showing light
On the bright side of the world
And the stone begins to burn

The stone begins to burn
Is that you, soul? Return
Is that you, soul? Return

The Offer

They made their highest offer on the house
The survey showed it was built on quarries
But they bought it anyway for the view.

The years brought shifts too small to be seen
Slipping right angles blurred by shadow
Fissures so fine they passed for webs –

Spasms on strings tugged by the streams that ran
Beneath them, turning up axes and rotting props
A sheep's skull, a rat's tail, a bird's beak –

Omens in the foundations that glowed at night
In bed when the off-balance buzzed in their ears
When they felt the earth adjust for hollow weight.

The collapse never came – they owned the threat of it
Like the snarling dog stopped by its chain. Theirs, too
The bricks around them, the space beneath them.

Ironing

You've just shaved and you smell of cream.
I'm watching you press the metal point
Between buttons, over a collar, into a seam.

When you've left, I open the wardrobe quietly –
I want to climb in and hang there with your shirts
With my creases, waiting for you to iron them out.

Map of the Moor

He's reading the map of the moor, under lowering clouds
Searching for paths trodden in by fearless men
Who found the first footholds on sliding scree
Sensed white stones in mist like a storm in the air –

Saying nothing of the path sunk into the bog and lost
He's thinking the sucking blackness firm, for her
He's making the dotted lines into stepping stones
For her feet to be safe on, making what should be, there.

Hope Street, 1966

They met for the first time by that radiator
In the Brahms section of the Philharmonic pub
(He told me). It was Hope Street, 1966.

She asked him where he came from
And he said – Over the Water –
Which she thought meant Poland (she told me)

Because of the black polo neck, the bag
Of herrings and rye bread from Poppa Volensky's –
How could she know he meant Rock Ferry?

She fought her corner – had to seal him to her
Nothing had ever been so important (she told me)
She was witty, beautiful, sharp (he told me). The rest

He choked on – just said when he walked her
Home past Sefton Park that night and kissed her
He knew he'd never let her go again.

Retirement

I could have looked forward to your white hair
The soft blue skirts of your old age
To fruit cake and tea by the fire.

You were looking forward to digging for hours
In the garden, your back elated by the sky –
Leaves in your hair and birds in your ears –

To plunging your hands into dark earth
Grasping some long white resisting root
Tapped in to the centre of the universe.

Month of Herons

A month of herons stood in flooded fields
Unshaken by the battering seconds of trains

Beaks raised, signs all pointing the same way
Accosting you with their rooted wood certainty –

Although their shape and colour are question marks
And one paused leg is lifted as a reminder

Of how long time can hang in the balance, how far
Mind can spread across the flat and silver water

They attend to with the attitudes of fishing rods
Owned by the hours before the fish is caught.

Yours is the spent second, bending branches,
Splitting silence – but these go back to being

As the train shuttles you on to your alarm clock.
Leaving the herons behind you think you're ahead but

The stillness they leave inside you belongs to mothers
Guarding the months you couldn't know were yours.

Exactly My Own Length

Exactly my own Length – there I lay and slept – It was quite soft.

Coleridge, Notebooks

If I'm allowed hope... No.
Hope *is* allowed – while we talk –
I hope for you one of those coffins
Found in evening light on a summer walk

Say a sheltering hollow in the heather
Marked by a wind-quiffed hawthorn
Rounded, sweetened and softened
By clumps of sheep wool and droppings
Where the ground is still herd-warm.

Or a shallow stickleback stream
Under the beeches in flickering light
On a bed of flat stones with the water's
Cool fingers untangling your hair
Until you're all flowing and green.

Or a long narrow gap in a smooth rock
Your own length, the fit exact
And soft enough to give up thought for sleep
With a sycamore tree to shade your face
A foxglove to flower at your feet.

One of those coffins that makes you think:
Here I'd be happy to stop a while
Here I've found the measure of my life
What else is there but sun and heather and bees?
What else could I be but part of This?

Although This is also the never-hoped-for
Slow-sucking bog on the darkening moor
That forces you to watch yourself slide
Feet first into its changeless archive
Of petrified time and trapped light.

Hope? The bog has no answer for the sea
That bides at the bottom of the combe
Has nothing to say to its tides and waves
Its colours and creatures, changing and free.

Book of Hours

But ours was to be a book of years –
Not months, not weeks, not days
Not minutes, which pass too fast to see.

Hours are no measure for our happiness
Let us at least have days
Let us have one per page.

In every frame a day of golden light
Look – you are smiling – dazed
By the brilliance of life.

I'll put years into the margins
Make decades of each leaf, each stream
Each forest thick with beasts.

I'll have the oceans there too, and the moon
The earth's red core, and cosmic string.

Each page so busy and thronging
We won't see the digits changing.

Laughter

There is morphine, which helps
But what we also have, for now
Is laughter.

Even if it does make your ribs hurt
At least you forget your back
At least you feel lighter.

For a moment
We flick jokes back and forth
About pain.

For a moment
Pain is a balloon bounced on our fingertips
Weighing almost nothing at all.

Sick World

...It means that the world is sound,
Whatever the sick microbe does. But he too is part of it.

Robinson Jeffers, De Rerum Virtute

World –
Whenever – from now on –
I see a quarry – a mine
A scar – a bruise on your surface
Something plundered – stolen
Taken – tainted – poisoned
Contaminated – spoiled
But still beautiful – still alive
I'll think of her
And mourn you both.

At the Door

At the door of this house
We need a box in which
To post our troubles as we arrive.

Troubles must not enter this house
Only lightness and smooth cheer
Bunches of gerberas and jokes.

If we're to keep up the walls of this house
Small things must not be made big
Big things must be made small.

The ticking bomb of this house
Is guarded by a sentry who may shout
To cover his deafness.

We who open the door of this house
Must enter stripped of clocks or watches –
Although you know what time it is.

At the door of this house
We need a box in which
To post our troubles as we leave.

Honouring the Dead

We spend an evening discussing ancestors
I'm taking notes and getting lost –

Great Granpa Jones, Bristol man, was really a Flanagan
On the run from the Black and Tans
Played the flute and said there were fairies in the phone
His son climbed up the gasworks after an air raid
And brought a bomb down the ladder in a bucket.

The other Great was Gentleman John Condon
Cattle drover, who ferried his beasts over
From Rosslare to the Great Western – it's late now
They all seem to have married each other's sisters –
Then there was the cousin who was a ragpicker…

You've decided they won't be forgotten
This is where you come from –
Not so much the people or the blood
As the talking, the telling, the making
Honouring the liveliness of the dead.

I'm afraid. How can your absence
Be imagined except as pain?

You Said This

There is nothing afterwards
You won't be fobbed off with eternity.

And why would it make things better
To know that others go on living
That they hold you in their minds?
When you're dead this means nothing.

Or to imagine your body will be earth
Provide food for some new tree?
What difference will it make
Once you are no longer Me?

No, it's not for the living
To make a fuss about grieving.
They're still here, still singing
They know who they are.

It's the dying must be allowed
To mourn their own departing.

The Weight of Life

You were reading
The weather in the streets
Olivia by Olivia.

You had cravings
For Terry's Bitter Orange Creams
And satsumas.

Your waters broke
In the Co-op on Cross Lane
After changing a tyre.

You gave me my life
At 1 a.m.
It weighed 6 pounds 11 ounces.

The Lovelace Place

In the cupboard in your room
Are the holly sticks he whittled
One each, in the woods above Culbone
On your Porlock honeymoon.

It was the day you headed up from the sea
Breathed on by waves and reciting trees
Onto the breast of the moor
Naming all the birds and flowers.

You found a ruined house up on the cliff
And on the clocktower carved in stone
Was what he swore would be his motto
— *Labour is its own reward* —

No More Fields

He will take her to see apples
In Somerset, in the autumn
He will carry her down the stairs
To sit in her garden
And listen to the leaves, the birds
She may even be able
To do some weeding...

Each time they say no.
He is crushed, then comes back:

If she can't travel in a car
He will hire an ambulance
A helicopter, a hot-air balloon
If she can't be carried
He will winch her down
The three floors from her window
If not autumn, then summer...

Each time they say no
But he does not hear.

When she stops taking morphine
When her creatin has gone down
When he has rubbed the muscle tone
Back into her legs
When she has built up her strength
With exercises he will give her
When she is eating properly again...

She looks up and shakes her head
– Don't clutch at straws –

Straws are all he has
Fieldfuls of stubble
Turning to dust
Hopes snapping endlessly underfoot
Re-forming as hydra-headed fire
How will he bear the black earth, on the day
When there are no more fields?

Stewed Fruit

He must be the one who brings her back to life
He's been in practice for some time now.

Stewing daily pans of fruit
Raspberries, blackberries, rhubarb
Rich and brilliant red lifeblood
Spilling into the white bowl
Staining her pale lips with health.

No pomegranate in his painting of the myth
Supermarkets sustain his endless summer.

A Request to the Cranes

Take her with you –
Bullet-bodied wind-backed birds
Let her feel the air
Filling her lungs
The cracks of her eyes
The space under arms, between fingers
Smoothing skin and sweeping back curls

Take her with you –
Show her the earth
Horses galloping, heather flashing
Herons dipping
Fly over lakes so smoothly
The surface mirrors your bellies
Steer her away from factories.

Be watchful – she's weak now
And may falter. Keep her awake
Lift her up with thermal breezes
Always fly in daylight zones
Let the hand of the sun be on her back
Fly low enough to cheat frost
Fly south and never know the Arctic.

Landing Light

All night you lurch
A ship of pain
With no harbour to head for
No friendly light
Except the one I wouldn't have you reach.

I must have a pillow ready for your head
Wherever it lands.

Transparent tubes and strings
Anchor you to life
Heavy machines and bags at the end of each
Whenever you move
I must stop them pulling out.

I'm just a helpless pair of hands
The lamp by your bed stays on all night.

Vigil

The wind moving through the aspens
The wind moving the clouds across the sky

The bed
The mirror over the sink
The chair by the window

The wind moving through
The wind moving the clouds

The bed
The clock on the wall
The mirror over the sink

The wind moving
The wind moving

The bed
The twisted sheets
The chair by the window

The wind
The wind

What To Do With a Baby

You're slipping away
I shouldn't ask this of you, but I do

– How will I know
What to do with a baby? –

You nod slightly, thinking
Then slip away slightly

Time passes, just me and the clock

Then you come back
Making an effort with the words

– What you do with babies is
You pat them

What you do with babies is
You love them

You'll know what to do –

I hold your bruised hand
As tightly as it can bear.

Fragile Domain

In this loaned hospital bed
She's at the mercy of us all
Dying is a fragile domain
To be entered with caution
Take your example from the nurses
Wear gloves or disinfect your hands
Look before you speak
Make your words honest
Keep your conclusions open
Be kind, be calm, be clear
Remove old dressings with a steady hand
Bring nothing with you into the room
But what you need for her
Do not litter it with yourself
Take nothing out of it
That does not belong to you.

Conversation

I know you can hear and every day now
We are living through the horror
Of the one-sided conversation.

Yesterday at least there were nods and shakes
The corner of a mouth turning up
Today even those are gone.

How can I never know what you think ever again?
My words are knocked back by my teeth
I leave you a silence you can't fill.

Nothing I Can Do

There is nothing I can do
I have fiddled with your pillows
Adjusted the angle of the bed
Stroked your head
Held your hand and hoped for a squeeze
Covered you with blankets
Taken them off again
Changed your sheets
Changed your nightie
Tried you with water
Milk tea coffee juice
Dabbed rosewater on your neck
Brushed your hair
Kissed your cheek
Talked to you
Asked you questions questions
Are you in pain
Are you worse
Are you comfortable
Are you okay
I don't know what the answer is
I tidy the pills you've stopped taking
I make a hot-water bottle for your feet
I put on some music
I light a candle
I hold your hand
I weep
There is nothing I can do.

All Souls' Day

I stand here in the ruins of your garden
In the dark
Searching for a last flower in bloom
To fill my empty hand
To fit the space between your fingers.
Wet leaves coat my shoes.

because there is nowhere you can be
    now
        no matter how much we want it
no one place that is you –
      although home is you
         love is you
         laughter is you

because there is nowhere your voice can be heard
    now
        no matter how we strain to hear it
no one voice that is yours
      although poplars are it
         grandmother is it
         singing along is it

because there is nothing for you to see
    now
        no matter how much we want to show you
no one thing that *is* because you see it
      although peonies flower
         babies are born
         mothers made

because your ashes are nothing but ash
    now
        no matter how we cling to them
there is this page
        on it some words
         never lapidary
         never enough

Last and First

...after the hard pain
of the last unsaid word...

Philip Levine

Comes the soft collapse of hope. But
Beyond the fumbled rite of forgiveness
Far from the crumpled sick-room bed
Shelved between the unbreathing walls
Of memory's cushioned cell

Written in the other-language of grief
The eye can rarely bear to decipher,
Is a book bound with such bitterness
Printed with such regret and remorse
Such night-waking recrimination and shame

It can only be read backwards
Leaving the last pages painfully behind
As a train slowly tracks the ragged outskirts
Of the city you hate to leave but must
The city you must live in but hate.

The years must be run alongside like rivers
The static canals of decades traced
Before you glimpse the first huddled bird
Before you see your breath turn to fog
Before you reach the white fields of snow

The second-chance pages where tears freeze
Before they can drop their stain, free
Of the black fingerpoints that show
Your heart where your hands have been −
And you were still allowed to live −

Here are whole pages where you are whole
So is she and you're smiling up at her eyes
Your small hand curled inside hers
Your palms both wrinkled by the same gene
Your fingers turning her fat wedding band.

She is singing to you – a little song
About something-to-pass-the-time
While the sun makes everything precious
Scatters light everywhere – glistening
The tips of your lashes, the points of leaves –

Streams from your chest pure as happiness
Into a world made of her magic – here –
You find the first word spoken in bliss
On the day when you first named her
When you belonged to each other gladly.

Selected titles from the Oxford*Poets* list

Oxford*Poets*, an imprint of Carcanet Press, celebrates the vitality and diversity of contemporary poetry in English.

Joseph Brodsky *Collected Poems In English*
For Brodsky, to be a poet was an absolute, a total necessity...scintillating deployment of language, and always tangential or odd ways of interpreting ideas, events or other literature. John Kinsella, OBSERVER

Carmen Bugan *Crossing the Carpathians*
To say these poems are beautiful is to risk underselling them. It is the specific nature of their beauty that matters, compounded as it is of dark experience, hope, magic, delight, generosity and love of language. George Szirtes

Greg Delanty *Collected Poems 1986–2006*
The fundamental tension that spurs Delanty's poetry crosses the domestic with the wayward, the retrospective with the prospective, and the result is a body of work that has grown steadily from book to book in depth, invention, and ambition. AGENDA

Jane Draycott *The Night Tree*
Hers is a scrupulous intelligence...Her searching curiosity and wonderful assurance make her an impeccable and central poetic intelligence. Penelope Shuttle, MANHATTAN REVIEW

Sasha Dugdale *The Estate*
Dugdale creates a spare, mythical tone that fits itself perfectly to the elemental Russian landscape in which much of her collection is set. GUARDIAN

Rebecca Elson *A Responsibility to Awe*
This is a wise and haunting volume, which I can't recommend too warmly. Boyd Tonkin, INDEPENDENT

Nigel Forde *A Map of the Territory*
Nigel Forde is a natural poet... It's obvious that both experience and thought make their impact on him in a rich mixture of imagery, rhythm and structure that enables them to be carried to us effortlessly. Arnold Wesker

Marilyn Hacker *Essays on Departure*
Everything is thrilling and true, fast and witty, deep and wise; her vitality is the pulse of life itself Derek Mahon

Anthony Hecht *Flight Among the Tombs*
Anthony Hecht's majestic development into a great poet has progressed across half-a-century. Flight Among the Tombs is his poignant and ironic masterpiece. Harold Bloom

Tim Kendall *Strange Land*
An intense and demanding collection. Its metaphysical honesty and its relevance demand our concentration. CHURCH TIMES

Jenny Lewis *Fathom*
The 'fathom' of Jenny Lewis's title
resounds through her collection as noun and
verb, implying both depth and the
reckoning of it…Her poems, in fact, employ
many of the techniques of painting, drawing
readers in through the gleam of colours so
intense and appealing as to be almost
edible. GUARDIAN

Lucy Newlyn *Ginnel*
Don't doubt that this is very good poetry
indeed…If you require a nostalgic hit of
childhood and place, the ingredients which
make this collection universal, it is here for
you. THE LEEDS GUIDE

Robert Saxton *Manganese*
Intellectually persuasive, tough-minded and
strikingly outspoken. This is an extremely
well-read, cultured poet…He is also one
heck of a craftsman, producing a dexterously
sculpted poetry. ORBIS

Peter Scupham *Collected Poems*
He writes wonderfully about places,
especially about English places…The
sophistication of the technique which
underpins every poem becomes clearer and
clearer as you read further in this
substantial, generous, distinguished volume.
Peter Davidson, Books of the Year
2005, READYSTEADYBOOK.COM

Joe Sheerin *Elves in the Wainscotting*
The Irish poet Joe Sheerin's superb second
collection… CITY LIFE

Penelope Shuttle *A Leaf Out of his Book*
Some of the poems are very funny…others
divertingly offbeat or simply moving…there
is a delight in the book as world, the world
as book. TIMES LITERARY SUPPLEMENT

Charles Tomlinson *Cracks In the Universe*
Tomlinson is a unique voice in contemporary
English poetry, and has been a satellite of
excellence for the past 50 years. David
Morley, GUARDIAN

Marina Tsvetaeva *Selected Poems*, trans. Elaine Feinstein
Marina Tsvetaeva was the first of the
modern Russian poets whose greatness
really came clear to me, thanks to these
translations. Feinstein has performed the
first, indispensable task of a great translator:
she has captured a voice. THREEPENNY
REVIEW

Chris Wallace-Crabbe *By and Large*
His allies are words, and he uses them with
the care of a surgeon and the flair of a
conjuror. Peter Porter